Fugitive Atlas

ALSO BY KHALED MATTAWA

Poetry

Mare Nostrum (Quarternote Chapbook Series)
Tocqueville
Amorisco
Zodiac of Echoes
Ismailia Eclipse

Criticism

How Long Have You Been with Us? Essays on Poetry
Mahmoud Darwish: The Poet's Art and His Nation

Translations of Arabic Poetry

Adonis, *Concerto al-Quds*
Amjad Nasser, *A Map of Signs and Scents: New and Selected Poems, 1979–2014*
    (cotranslated with Fady Joudah)
Adonis, *Selected Poems*
Amjad Nasser, *Shepherd of Solitude: Selected Poems*
Joumana Haddad, *Invitation to a Secret Feast*
Iman Mersal, *These Are Not Oranges, My Love: Selected Poems*
Maram Al-Massri, *A Red Cherry on a White-tiled Floor: Selected Poems*
Fadhil Al-Azzawi, *Miracle Maker: Selected Poems*
Saadi Youssef, *Without an Alphabet, Without a Face: Selected Poems*
Fadhil Al-Azzawi, *In Every Well a Joseph Is Weeping*
Hatif Janabi, *Questions and Their Retinue: Selected Poems*

Anthologies of Arab American Literature

Beyond Memory: An Anthology of Contemporary Arab American Creative Nonfiction
    (coedited with Pauline Kaldas)
Dinarzad's Children: An Anthology of Contemporary Arab American Fiction
    (coedited with Pauline Kaldas)
Post Gibran: Anthology of New Arab American Writing
    (coedited with Munir Akash)

Fugitive Atlas

Poems

Khaled Mattawa

Graywolf Press

This publication is made possible, in part, by the voters of Minnesota through a Minnesota State Arts Board Operating Support grant, thanks to a legislative appropriation from the arts and cultural heritage fund. Significant support has also been provided by Target Foundation, the McKnight Foundation, the Lannan Foundation, the Amazon Literary Partnership, and other generous contributions from foundations, corporations, and individuals. To these organizations and individuals we offer our heartfelt thanks.

Published by Graywolf Press
250 Third Avenue North, Suite 600
Minneapolis, Minnesota 55401

www.graywolfpress.org

Published in the United States of America

ISBN 978-1-64445-037-6

2 4 6 8 9 7 5 3 1
First Graywolf Printing, 2020

Library of Congress Control Number: 2019956914

Cover design: Mary Austin Speaker

Cover photo: US Department of the Interior and US Geological Survey, *Eerie Cloud Shadows* (southern Egypt). Landsat 8, March 22, 2014.

For Reem and Salma,
beloved companions in dark times.

CONTENTS

IV. *Fugitive Atlas*

V.

Once more the storm is rising from fate's black quarter.
The mind feels faint,
bemused like a body turned inside out.
Who is that dancing in the bats'-wing cloak?
Who was struck dumb by the rattle of what he saw?

Vladimír Holan

Traveler, nomad, hoarder of perceptions,
you have no guide but the eyes of speech.

Ahmed Fouad Negm

Fugitive Atlas

TAPROOT AND CRADLE

Evening coffee, and my mother salts
her evening broth—not equanimity
but the nick of her wrist—

and my mother bakes bread,
and my mother hobbles, knees locked,
and my mother carries the soft stones of her years.

O pen of late arrivals.
O knife of darkened temples.
O my scurrying, my drunken snakes.

I deliver her to the earth under summer rain.
I remember the killed enemy.
I remember my good friends.

I.

BEATITUDE

*We did indeed offer the amanah to the Heavens, Earth and Mountains;
but they refused it, being afraid thereof: but man took it for he indeed
was foolish and unjust.* The Quran 33:72

My child wants to know if the mountains really cowered.

How do you know when a sea or a river is afraid?

How do you know when the sky is thinking yes or no?

And him, why did he say yes? Did he know

that all the other creatures refused the burden?

That he was God's last choice?

SHIKWAH

—After Muhammad Iqbal

Brother on the threshing floor, body like wheat,
and the red dirt that binds us. The fig trees, olives
and date palms, the treacherous murder unleashed

upon us now, the call blazing from vanity's lungs,
jutting us to a future of mindless rain, wayward blizzards
of sand and snow. We were born to ward off this desolation

that grinds mountains into floss, that bores into our books
for a whim that ordains blood, our blood
and others', our sisters', mothers'. Without such fear,

such hope, who will we be? What will we do without
this aching chord, without the bright morning that tore
silver's towers? Fire and the parched red dirt

that binds, the water stolen from our wells,
a black magic dredging the lower rungs of earth.
We dream of clover. The soft scent of young lambs

is the first letter of our alphabet, and the prophets
who tighten ropes around their waists to stifle hunger's
pangs, supplicant brows seeking light from earth's core.

What will we do without the angel's voice, a tide
sending us heavenward, a harmattan ushering us into the hell
of its lows? How can we accept the quiet certainty of our graves?

There must be shelter, we whisper to each other, beyond
the sun's hardened gaze, an opening through the moonlit
canopy of fronds where signs alight and prayers launch.

The girls walk past, hair fluttering like commas
between poems of musk, a dream of touch like water
gently falling on smooth, warm stone. Dusk commences,

brings back the anemones' mournful dirge stroking
the dagger's spine and the gelding's nightmares. Our love
for the gaze that lingers only for our eyes is all that remains

in our scoured hands. Who else will hear birdsong
as prayer, who will cleanse himself with the stroke
of sand? Who keeps the earth rotating with praise

of your name? And what will this spinning,
hurtling mean without our voices shouldering it
toward some ripe, sweetened pause?

What will you do, dear God, without us? How
will you fare, alone again in the empty vast, in the dark
of your creation, without us giving you your name?

A DREAM OF ADAM

One afternoon in autumn I find him in the backyard trying to shelter himself from the rain. Disheveled and exhausted, he reminds me so much of Márquez's old man with enormous wings that I half expect to see feathers on his back. His long hair falls in white, thin strands smeared with mud, and his wet, matted beard barely hides his sunken cheeks. He refuses to come inside when I invite him in, only asks for a hot drink, "with something in it, please!" When I return with tea spiked with rum, he holds the mug with both hands and brings it close to his chest. "Sit down," he tells me, "I need to rest here for a little bit." I set my chair next to his and he begins talking, his words interrupted by coughs, grunts, and long sighs. He talks all night through my sleep.

> At the world's quiet
> end, Adam's yearning. Not for
> heaven, only to
>
> ask, "Why did thee from clay
>   mould me,
> from darkness promote me?"

ANTHROPOCENE HYMNS

1.

The need for armaments
as the world is remade in words
floating above the still waters.

A fellow tribesman surveys the field for a hunt,
seeking grasslands for grazing,
or a place to sleep among the trees.

The air smells of pig,
geysers spray, and miniature rainbows
ripple above a lagoon.

2.

The down of our nests, concrete and plastic.
The project almost completed,
taken over two million acres of desert lands.

Thousands of apartment blocks
awaiting further procreation.
The body politic must live without water now.

3.

Churn that spins and flows.
The rumble of chains, the grind of confession:
a tightening of the body's circuitry.

4.

What is the difference between wolf and fox
in the homeland? Is it possible for a bird
to be two birds, or four lizards?

Some rise at daybreak, others hunt at night.
A churn at the level of sea and moon,
wolves and foxes, birds and lizards.

But not a churn in the absolute.
That would come later, that and the idea of value.
An evolution of traps and scalping.

5.

A clearing.
A flatness that is no longer a field,
a burning plate exhaling its dust.

6.

A copulation between these two verbs,
learn and *adapt*,
between two concrete towers collapsing.

7.

The seasons are at work on everything,
even on themselves, an extinction here, a mutation there,
some sort of algae blocking the stream, suffocating the fish—

the insects whose excrement
is turning the Taj Mahal green—
to become a necessity,

a new organic machine
that separates flight from body
and reserves the motions in pixels for reuse.

8.

You recall a certain hope
as something so small that it can fit
into a postcard of your hometown.

In the long exposure
the boulevard is streaked with car lights,
red going one way, white going the other.

9.

To be alive then, with meaning, in a far corner
from one's thoughts and beliefs,
to be nonhuman, nonbird—

we have not gotten there yet.
How to stop thinking of bodies
as worth extinction, worth eating or enslaving—

brought to whip or firing squad.
The hovel, the burrow,
the hive grown thin—

concrete with bones and hair mixed in.
A history enfolding words nourished on blood.
Don't tell me we are not who we are.

10.

The theater inside the churn,
inside the big human cave,
a faint smell of pig wafts through the vents.

The chains await us like airplane seatbelts.
No place else to go.
Nowhere but this earth.

SEASON OF MIGRATION TO THE NORTH

You climb wheezing, choking
on Addis air; then you find yourself
in these scented woods.

Backbreaking, but I love bundling
the leaves, how the rain soaks
the scent into your clothes and skin.

Seven years gathering eucalyptus leaves
from King Menelik's forests—their fire
makes the best injera, I'm told.

Maybe that's why Menelik built
his palace here, a great church looming
over it to show he was content.

But even he was tempted away;
his queen sent a messenger from the foot
of Entoto saying she's found a new (addis)

flower (ababa), and he followed her
like Adam out of paradise
to cofound the metropolis nightmare.

Was my dream worth more than enough
air to live on, something between
banal sin and the creator's potency?

Addis to the source of the Nile,
then Khartoum to Sinai, to be
an asylee in Tel Aviv, or northwest

through Darfur and Sabha,
to the Bride of the Med. Names
like shabby trees on a map,

lines for a screen where bodies
are stick figures dancing
to tepid applause. Each a degree

in a circle inside a void, unmarked
time, days like scentless leaves
that slip through your hands.

PLUME

Deep under the affluent college town where I live, an hour from Flint, Michigan, there is a moving plume of groundwater contaminated with 1,4-dioxane. The chemical ended up in the water table when a local manufacturer dumped large quantities of it into the ground. "A known human carcinogen," 1,4-dioxane is a colorless liquid with a faint, sweet smell. Brief exposure to it can irritate the eyes and the respiratory tract, while repeated exposure can damage the central nervous system, liver, and kidneys. The chemical does not readily bind to soils, and quickly leaches to groundwater. Dioxane in surface soil can take up to fifteen years to degrade to half its concentration. In deeper soil, it will remain virtually unchanged.

Our plume had spread through the groundwater of the surrounding townships, forcing the closure of private wells, and is now edging closer to our city's main water supply, Barton Pond. Local environmental authorities report that they have detected dioxane in the lake. The manufacturer who originally dumped the chemical is still fighting litigation in court as the plume continues to spread.

I'm still taken by the word *plume*. I can't erase the associations it has with Carnival, flapper fashion, Cyrano de Bergerac's hat, and the ostrich feather fans of my childhood. In our local context, the word has begun to refer almost exclusively to the dioxane under us, not that we talk about it much. In newspapers and on the internet, maps of the hundreds of underground water contamination sites in the US consistently portray plumes as giant colorful feather shapes, some pointed and sleek, others fluffy and plump.

Angels, crimson, blue,
and gold, draped in poisoned quills,
ghosting the dusk below

the hours, let not your
fiery water
inflict upon us.

'ALAMS FOR SAYING "YES"

noted the distance
   how far you and I
      from the loop

now a voice coos
   into the night
      what to say to it

how does it find us
   this longing
      this hunger shaking

ever homeward
   we've lived
      in the recesses

what will it ask
   of us
      this kind shadow

are we even alive
   we crawl through
      the trees

how long
   like a pair of wings
      separately together

into the eye
   of the sun
      in the dark

when we rise
   from the tunnels
      under our sleep

II.

UNREAL CITY

How would I return? After all that happened, I'd choose to be like I was: a stubborn thing. No, not a rat or a cockroach. I mean something that has beauty about it. Maybe that's what perseverance is, to allow yourself to be pulled by some notion of the mind, away from yourself.

Sometimes for comfort, I think of myself as a field. I lie fallow and nurse the life within me. Or like a city that can be rebuilt again. Poets would sing of my river and of my roads as veins coming to life. I have been a city, of course, a city that has kept a secret hurt under it, and in the dredging of renewal, of towers and tunnels, secrets emerge, stark and horrifying.

What happened to me? It's what has happened to women and cities in war—and in peace too—when life turns against itself. And who is to blame? There's isn't one notion of purity that has not ravished me, not a single notion of kinship, faith, or honor that has not dug its dagger into me. And as ever, it's the strong pummeling the weak and showing little charity.

I would want to return to whittle at the damage, and to have what I was denied. Sometimes I think I would rather live for thinking alone—my crude function lost to me—and when beauty fades, I'll never know what it means to have had anything. I can only think of what I'd like to happen, something postponed but vivid in the mind. That's all.

> They crawled death's ditches, tore
> birth canals—their songs spread a
> sheen of triumph on loss—
>
> it's only her grief that can
> cleanse
> the stones' thoughts, the veins of the stars.

OCCUPATION: AN INDEX

A

A day's living—
hands' cunning
drained

A murdered son
for cameras
to retain

A slave
who has made
a mistake

A song made
to induce
survival

A taker with
no pang
of guilt

A victim,
it's your turn
now

Air that shepherds
jet fighters,
missiles, drones

Amicable people
with whom we are
on equal terms

Amused our-
selves counting
the dead

An apricot tree
laden
with fruit

And the pastures
at Lafwat
bursting green

Armed
vehicles, tanks,
crushed cars

Arms bound,
patience withers,
no livelihood

As if the land
had no
people

Ask no questions
and you'll hear
no lies

At the shiver
of spring
in the grass

B

Barbed wire
looped around
huts and tents

Bestial sexual
license (of occupied
people)

Blaring from
the soldiers'
loudspeakers

Brainless
elites, degraded
masses

Breaking
of fingers
and knees

Bulldozers
cut down a row
of cypresses

Burnt corpses
on both sides
of the road

Burying
the living
for sport

C

Carrying filth,
wood and water—
a low life indeed

Carrying on
as if free
of disease

Chased them
from before
the city gate

Climb back
to the clouds,
O beloved water

D

Degenerates
who deserve to
be conquered

Destroyed all
that belongs
to their jinn

Dig out their
olive trees, burn
their lentil fields

Disfigure past
to paralyze
imagination

Dreams that
pine for
lost sleep

Drink you in
heaving gulps,
beloved water

E

Entropy
undertaken
with courage

Essential duplicity
(of occupied
people)

Even managed
to defecate into a
photocopier

Every day a story
about why they're
killing you

Exchanged
in a market
of guilt

F

Finish the
population
exchange

For months
the curfew
closes doors

For weeks
for four or five
hours a day

Force is
all they ever
understand

Forced to leave
homes, move in
with family

Forgive them
for forcing us to
kill their children

G

Garments up
around their
waists

Gunned down
in the forced
labor camp

H

How do
you master
innocence

How do you
spin your
pleading

How high
must the
walls rise

How long will
the roads be
yours alone

How long will
you wish they'd
just disappear

How will you
explain to
your children

How you've
crept into
our lungs

I

I have no
illness but
this place

I myself had
to become
a weapon

I remember
those places,
forget my loss

I wish
I were
there now

If I were one
of them, I'd be
a terrorist too

If you
deserve our
confidence

I'll be grateful
to reach them
alive

Imprisoned
clan, banished
kin's abode

In drawers
they pulled
out of desks

Into plastic
bags, they
scattered

J

Jailing
by old
Jailliol

Joints of their
limbs like knots
in a rope

Jolly
pioneers
of progress

Joy, sorrow,
devotion,
rage

Just an accident
arising from the
weakness of others

Just as though
a mission
to civilize you

Just robbery
and murder
on a grand scale

Just the thought
of their
humanity

K

Keep
hope
intact

Keep plunder
and livestock
for yourself

L

Like drugged
cockroaches
in a bottle

Lives lost
before
my eyes

M

Malnutrition
permanently
introduced

Man who
wants to move
forward

Many
without
a story

Millions
torn from
their gods

Monster, the
everyday
monster

More effective
and efficient
tyranny

Most
unscrupulous
financiers

Must believe
myself
superior

Mutual
services
and complicity

N

Neighborhood
dogs join
in the ruckus

No colonization
without eviction
and expropriation

No illness but
a providence
of grief

No illness but
"Beat them
no pardon"

No illness but
the drip
of loss

Not one
drop
of blood

Not one
effort, not one
privation

Not only
pathological
but pathogenic

Now a field
hand on my
own land

Now a morsel
to shove down
a throat

O

O civilization—
innocence
misunderstood

O killer,
needful
of dead love

On children's
hair, faces,
into their mouths

On the floors,
in emptied
flowerpots

Open hands
snuffed out
like flames

Open hands
that kept
opening

P

Perform
your ablutions
then return

Pioneers
who deserve
admiration

Pioneers who
made the
desert green

Propensity for
violence (among
occupied people)

Puddles hold
and gusts of
wind release

Q
Questions in
the interests
of science

Quick glance
of unconcerned
wisdom

Quickly enough
when the flesh
falls off

Quirky tweaking
of our private
will

R
Remains of
a suicide
bomber

S
Sacrifice
given despite
perseverance

Sandbag
terraces,
hunker down

Scattered
in cardboard
boxes

Set it on
fire when
you're done

Silver and
gold, trays
of brass

Soldiers' piss
like blood,
falling warm

T
The bullet
in her riddled
heart

The crowning
glory of
our genius

The rot
of loved ones'
corpses

The soldiers
take over
the roof

Their orange
groves
burned

There are no
innocents
here

They defecate
in kitchen sinks,
in pots and pans

They defecate
on computers,
on children's beds

They want you
to bow like
a slave

This is how
you make
the land yours

This is
policy not
a joke

To bring you
up to
modernity

To drive
them out of
our memories

To make
you a new
nation

Truth
stripped of its
cloak of time

U

Uproot their
pomegranate
trees

Urinated into
their drinking
water tank

V

Verging on tears,
he knew
it was a lie

Vets describe
a dark, depraved
enterprise

Vivid, on-the-
record accounts
of slaughter

Voice changed, said:
"We must talk like
civilized people"

Voices that seemed
suspiciously
innocent

W

Watch your
injury spun
into blame

When your
conscience
is naught

Where your
pain is
priced low

Whimpers
for mercy
into claws

X

X drawn on
homes to be
demolished

X equals
my right name
and address

Y

You are
drenched, but
you've survived

You become the
cause and effect of
their oppression

You vow again
never to leave
it to them

Z

Zealous
patience to heap
and hoard

Zenith to
nadir till
the end

Zero-
tolerance
policy

Zigzagged
between the
snipers' crosshairs

OUR NEIGHBORS: POISONED CITY

In April 2014 the Michigan state government changed the City of Flint's water source to the nearby Flint River. Shortly thereafter, there was not only more lead coming out of the city's taps, but also more lead in the blood of the city's children. In just eighteen months, the percentage of children under age five with high blood-lead levels had jumped from 2.1 percent to 4 percent. When the physician who made the discovery looked at the two zip codes with the highest levels of lead in their water, she saw that there was even greater harm. There, the proportion of children with high blood-lead levels rose to 6.3 percent. Both were mostly poor areas with large African American populations, 67 percent and 46 percent respectively. Altogether, there were as many as 27,000 children vulnerable to persistent lead exposure.

The switch to the Flint River happened despite the fact that people knew the river to be highly contaminated. When the state government began talking of using it as their city's new source of drinking water, "we thought it was a joke," said one citizen. A pastor in the city testified that over at his church, they had stopped using the river for baptisms years ago.

> To rivers where souls
> slake their thirst, where infants
> bathe in your bitter facts
>
> and deceitful wiles, how long
> will the poison
> of your green eyes flow?

FACE

—To the One Million Plus

1.

It's true, we've gotten used to your absent faces,
while the soldiers are enumerated, name, age,
sex, branch of service, cause of death.

How did you die?
Who buried you and how?
Are you in heaven now, are you still waiting?

Do your children or parents still remember you?
Does the dirt know you? The water drink you?
Do lavender and clematis still shoot out of your remains?

2.

A photo of a bride and groom:
He is a veteran Marine.
His nose is flattened into two holes

in the middle of his face. There are no ears.
Gleaming skin covers the whole of his skull.
No eyelashes, no eyebrows.

Some of the mouth had been recovered
after dozens of surgeries to repair him.
His eyes peer at her through two slits.

She must have looked at him this way numerous times
and turned away, but she can't do that now:
the picture must be taken for the world to see.

Why can't she give up this man who was
perhaps handsome and kind? Give him back
to those who sent him away, tell them,

"You take him! Why must I be the one
who has to wake up to this horror every morning?
Why do I have to face it alone?"

He turns to kiss her with his nonexistent lips,
leans into her, gratified for the safety
he finds there. She stands, eyes unmoving.

3.

And now you, O million plus,
how many of you are still burning?
This wasteland is all yours now.

What will it be: a country, a state, a territory?
And what will you be: a nation,
a faith, a sect? Unschooled

and countless like dust, we must find
a new symbol, a new divinity to bind you
and cover your missing limbs.

4.

We welcome another
goddess, we'll add her
to our pantheon,

they say. But how to tell
of the uranium in her
water and dirt, and what

to name the writhing
in her belly, the babies
born with two heads?

You must help us
fit her in the stories
we know. This symbol,

this mother
sheltering us in the tent
of her meaning.

5.

Every second a face,
the sixty in a minute,
the billion in a projected life,

each one a face
—the apparition of these—
the ones passing and living between,

each a face,
and I look at hers, my daughter's,
held in my hands,

how when sleeping beside me
she'd take my hand
and place it on her face.

She is the echo that sings them
all together, a clot
and its infinitesimal divisions

chanting the name
of the species
through the alleys of my veins.

Seconds and faces intertwined,
almost redeeming,
held my hand asking

if we can go
to the park
this afternoon,

as if time can still guide me,
as if I can still face
the world I'm leaving her.

6.

When—after the long wait—you come
to rescue me, love, the million plus
will be my selves, my others,

the pores on my skin, the hair on my head.
They'll be my eyelashes and eyebrows—
the signature of God on my face.

Perhaps I'll no longer have to find you
like a path through a minefield then,
or a shadow lost to the dimming dusk.

You will tell me
whose forgiveness to seek,
what I must not touch, see, or believe.

You'll tell me, won't you, love,
what all my yielding
will finally yield.

7.

You have already freed me.
You have taken your revenge.
Why have you come again, my brother?

We had no choice how time joined us,
you say. We're no longer
aggressor or victim, you insist.

We're the faces on the new currency, traded
in ways beyond our reckoning.
We must work together, you explain.

Remember, when you blew up these houses,
these bridges, hospitals, schools?
Wasn't I alive then, and weren't you?

But now you talk of the future,
and you look at my face
as if you still have one.

8.

So, what happened to our brother,
the soldier with the lost face, the one
whose wedding was attended by senators and governors,

the one whose disfigurement was the price
of courage, love, and sacrifice?
Where is he now?

Did we really expect the marriage to last,
that he would prosper, that she would stay?
When we found him one January night,

facedown on hard snow,
dead from booze and meth,
were we really surprised?

9.

How will I ever see you again,
my love? Their flashlights,
their cameras, their bombs,

and their records of us, microscopes,
satellites that strip us
to the secret braid of our breath.

Oh, they know so much. Our future
is blotted with pools of light,
and we have drowned in their knowing.

Hasn't light done enough to us?
The inhuman light of the mighty,
the desperate light of the dispossessed

have rendered us gleaming like sand.
How do I cull you now, my love,
from among a million shatterings?

Turn off the light.
Let me see your face
in the dark.

10.

No ideas, no conceits, only the weight
of things, the fate of things,
the card you carry that has no face.

Something must be in my bones
that makes them brittle, swept
by the wind like straw or grass.

Something in my blood, how it seeps
out of me and dries out like leather
in the sun. Or in my flesh,

some mistaken fuse that makes it want
to explode into a million faces,
in multiplicities of longing and loss.

I see my body shaped in shadow,
feel it struck down against the ground,
whole and enduring—woman

like other women, man like other men—
clinging to its breath, seeking its one face
reflected in the changing sky.

AN IDEA FOR A SHORT FILM

I imagine writing a screenplay of a short film for my friend, the Egyptian filmmaker Tamer El Said. I doubt that he will want to make this film, but I've written a treatment just in case.

In scene 1, Prometheus lines up the men he's made out of clay and places them on a hill above a valley. He asks Zephyros for rain and watches as his creations dissolve and trickle into the river.

Scene 2 requires a screen split four ways. On screen 1, the Chinese goddess Nuwa pounds the molded figures she's made out of yellow earth into flat circles like pancakes. On screen 2, the Sumerian earth goddess Ninhursag, like a wine presser, stands in a giant vat pounding the human shapes she'd made into a giant lump of clay. On screen 3, Ea, the Akkadian god, tosses human clay figures into the Tigris as if tossing bread to fish and ducks in a pond. On screen 4, the Yoruba god Obatala is tucking human-shaped lumps, like wedges of yam, into the soil from which he made them. The simultaneous movements in the four screens should bring to mind propaganda footage of factory workers at wartime.

Single screen again in scene 3. The Hindu goddess Parvati is shown moving her brush in deliberate strokes—as if the film is being played backward—to remove the blue patina from her son Ganesh, whom she'd made from clay. The scene ends with her tearing off his fingers and toes.

Split screen for scene 4. Yahweh and the Maori god Tāne are pulling back the breath they'd blown into the nostrils of the first man and woman they'd made respectively. The breaths should look like white ribbons at first but grow into clouds as more is pulled out.

As scene 5, I suggest to Tamer that we "must do our best to film it in Luxor despite the risks and the censorship." Here, the god Unkh reaches inside human wombs. He pulls us out, we the pieces of clay he'd once placed there.

> When I compounded am with clay,
> what of love to claim my defense,
> what from beauty but remorse?
>
> Only time will have its say,
> the so much
> lived, the unrehearsed.

III.

BEATITUDE

Did you really have a party the day the dictator died?

And you had a cake decorated with all the flags?

Did you think his death will fix everything?

Why did we spend all that time there?

And all these people fighting, fleeing,

and drowning, what are they hoping for?

'ALAMS FROM THE BLACK HORSE PRISON, TRIPOLI, CIRCA 1981

—For Mohammed El-Mufti and in memory of Muhammed Al-Shaltami

barely a man
   leaving behind
      this forlorn town

with strangers
   I was a lame bird
      I dreamt up glory

home once again
   who won't abide
      despoiling

soon they'll try
   to kill me
      set my house ablaze

when I traveled
   memory shielded
      a feeble flame

poor starving creatures
   brooding nest-bound
      a sign from fate

with my brothers
   their poisoning
      the ground

must I stay put
   is it up to me again
      my life a ransom

far up north
   muddled longings
      I wore like a crown

scattered among rocks
   plotting my return
      to my native town

I'm their enemy
   who must atone for
      all their crimes

a prisoner how long
   must my heart beat
      to redeem this ground

A STORY

I told the boy, "Once there was
a bird," and he said, "What is
a bird?" I told the boy,

"There was this tree," and he said,
"What is a tree?" The mother
was in a corner of the cell,

hugging her knees, but the boy
looked on. His face and hands
clean, his hair trimmed.

That day the guard took me
out of my cell, brought me to them
and said, "Tell this boy a story."

He used to beat me whenever
I said my name. "You're just
a number here," he'd say,

striking my face with a hose.
Then something made him kinder.
He brought me an apple, some grapes

every now and then, even a nail
clipper once. That night, we walked
silently through the corridors—

he didn't want his boss to know—
and he opened their cell.
So I sang the boy some songs.

He stared at me, not saying
a word; his young mother
looked away, started to convulse.

I knocked on the bars of their cell
for the guard to let me out. "I can't
breathe here!" I hissed at him.

She was in college when they brought
her to jail to punish her father,
a dissident, who fled the country.

They raped her and she had the boy
in that same cell. He'd never seen
the sun, or kicked a ball or sat

in the shade of a tree. Back in my cell
I told the guard, "I can't tell that boy anything.
Don't ever take me there again."

"But you're an intellectual," he said.
"That's your duty. You must try."
I couldn't tell if he'd found another way

to torment me, or if he really wanted
to help the boy. After that night,
I never saw any of them again.

NOW THAT WE HAVE TASTED HOPE

—An Anthem

Now that we have come out of hiding,
why would we live again in the tombs
we'd made out of our souls?

And the sundered bodies that we've reassembled
with prayers and consolations,
what would their torn parts be other than flesh?

Now that we have tasted hope
and dressed each other's wounds
with the legends of our oneness,

would we not prefer to close our mouths
forever shut on the wine
that swilled inside them?

Having dreamed the same dream,
having found the water that gushed
behind a thousand mirages,

why would we hide from the sun again
or fear the night sky after we've reached the ends of darkness,
live in death again after all the life our dead have given us?

Listen to me cities, houses, alleys,
courtyards, and streets that throng my veins,
some day soon

in your freed light and in the shade of your proud trees,
your excavated heroes will return to their thrones.
Lovers will hold each other's hands as if they'd never known fear.

I need not look far to imagine the nerves
dying, rejecting the life that blood sends them.
I need not look deep into my past to seek a thousand hopeless vistas.

But now that I have tasted hope,
I have fallen into the embrace
of my own rugged innocence.

How long were my ancient days?
I no longer care to count.
How high were the mountains in my ocean's fathoms?

I no longer care to measure.
How bitter was the bread of bitterness?
I no longer care to recall.

Now that we have tasted hope,
now that we have lived on this hard-earned crust,
we would sooner die than seek any other taste to life.

AFTER 42 YEARS

Five years old when the dictator took over in a coup—
curfew shut our city down.
Bloodless coup, they said.

The dictator, a young man,
a shy recluse, bent in piety,
the dead sun of megalomania hidden in his eyes.

Could not go to the store to buy bread or milk,
could not leave home, visit friends, the radio
thundering hatred, retching blood-curdling songs.

Decades on—factories built and filched, houses stolen, newspapers shut down,
decades of people killed,
42 years.

But that's all over now—
How can you say over when it took 42 years—
I was five when the dictator took my brother away.

Over now—42 years—must look ahead.
His face half blood-covered, half smirking,
hands raised, fingers pressed together upward saying,

wait,
calm down, wait.
Wait 42 years.

Bloodless coup, the country like a helpless teenage girl
forced into marriage
hoping her groom will be kind.

In between there was blankness
that burned a million suns into our eyes,
death like air, everywhere.

What was it like to be held by his men?
Fingernails pulled out, testicles fried,
hung from a clothesline rope, the dictator's mistress pulling at my legs?

How many killed—the cracked skulls, the mass graves, the uncounted dead?
Five years old
when my father was killed standing in front of a hotel smoking a cigarette.

Who taught you, sons of my country, to be so fearless and cruel?
Him, they say, for 42 years, 42 years of him.
Who taught you to treat a human being like this?

The no-life we had to live,
under him,
the lives we were asked to live as dead.

Alive, we want him alive, they kept shouting.
To make him taste their bitterness and rage?
Alive, alive!

GAME OVER—
Allahu Akbar!
GAME OVER—with the capture of a 69-year-old rat?

The night-game of breaking into houses, arresting dozens; the day-game of civility—
We'll bring him in a few hours.
We'll bring him back in 42 years.

A clown in a rat-colored outfit, a wild mop of hair, a wig,
holding a golden pistol like a boy playing hero, high-heeled boots.
Is that what our history amounted to?

There were suns that would never light.
There were holes in the air that was full of death.
We managed to hold our breath and live our lives.

But how do we end an epoch then?
The crammed jails, the torture, bodies left hanging in public squares.
The mind-twisting corruption, the roving sense of dread, the waste.

How do we know
who we are,
or what we can become?

I was five when my brother disappeared,
I was 13, I was 20, I was 76,
I was never allowed to reach birth.

What will be our aftermath?
One minute
and all of that history is found hiding like a rat.

The horror of seeing history become history,
caught in a flood drain,
the pain too dark to bear, the light burning cold.

He died of his wounds.
What wounds?
They just shot him dead.

He was a magnet that drew evil out of men's chests,
his hands, his hands saying *wait, wait*,
reached into their lungs and knotted their raw souls.

No, no,
they just shot him dead.
But I heard he died of his wounds.

Too much for a young man who could not stop killing again.
To tear him to bits, my mother's friend once said,
to tear him to bits, millions had prayed.

One bullet, or two,
some say three,
despite the pleading fingers tainted with their own blood.

He looks at them
as if he'd never seen or heard of blood,
surprised that he too would bleed if cut.

One bullet,
two,
or three,

history is captured, a knife thrust into his rectum
and he falls, kicked about and shot in the head.
History tossed into a freezer, put on display.

Lord, how little our lives must be,
when so much can be buried lost,
dumped in a hole, forgotten dust!

What will
our aftermath
be then?

We wash our hands,
put on spotless clothes.
There is no "after" until we pray for all the dead.

YOUR CITY

In your Cairo, Tamer, the generals fear another revolt. They are planning to abandon the city and are building a new capital in the middle of the desert to house all the government's thirty ministries and their staff. Everything in the new capital will be the tallest or largest in the Middle East and Africa. It will have a new airport, a monorail, hundreds of colleges, hospitals, and schools, forty thousand hotel rooms, a theme park four times the size of Disneyland, sensors for pollution, sensors for speed, and huge solar-energy farms. The plans do not include low-income housing, but certainly thousands of facial-recognition cameras to track and arrest potential troublemakers. The project will occupy six million acres of desert land. It will siphon water that had been slotted for other towns.

Where sands stretch far
away, Adam stands, thronged by
guards, adoring his towers;

his slaves milk his lean cows,
feed on
hard bread and brackish water.

AFTER 42 YEARS (REVISITED)

How cruel humans
        can be when they become
a violent

                                                    What to say to those
                                                    who call his days "the beautiful
                                                        epoch," who think

                        it's worse
                        than you
                        think

tyrannical mob!
        Oh what a torrent! A deluge
that has no mercy

                                                    him a great man—had
                                                    people's welfare at heart—
                                                        father to the nation—

                        you dreamers
                        were
                        fooled

for those who stand in
        its way, heedless of those
crying from pain, never

                                                    who say, "we don't need
                                                    freedom—we need a tyrant
                                                        just like him again."

                        and you
                        fooled
                        us

extending a hand
        to help. Rather it
pushes them down into

                                                    This is what happens
                                                    when abasement and trauma
                                                        are twisted into

                        we used
                        to have
                        a country

the abyss without
        a care. Thus, the tyranny
of a single man is

                                                    nostalgia. That's all
                                                    the sweetness they can hatch out
                                                        of paralysis.

now we've
lost our
homes

the most tolerable of
*   tyrannies; after all, he*
is just one man

Then there are the ones
who can't stop killing, seeking
old and new enemies.

the decency
of regular
salaries

and can be removed
*   from power by the nation,*
even by one of

Young people who can't
tell virtue from crime and for
whom violence has

we
sleep
in tents

its imbeciles with
*   a single blow. The tyranny*
of the mob is

become the only
justification for their
lives. Their eyes betray

our children
beg and
starve

the worst form of
*   oppression. Who can stand in*
the face of a sweeping

a panic that doubles
as a savage joy, a force
pushing them toward

we didn't
know we
were happy

torrent, its blind and
*   overwhelming power? Oh*
how I love the freedom

more slaughter, a lost
glory that flashes like a
mirage among

                    as far
                    as happiness
                    went

of the masses, when   the ruins they create.
    they thrust forward without   A generation who will
a master, freed from   devour each other. It's

                    it's all
                    gone
                    now

their chains. But Oh how   the ones who know none
    I fear and suspect them, how   of this terrible history
they fill me with dread.   who will save us.

MY CITY

And now to my disheveled city, which lit up in rebellion, then turned on itself with assassinations and riots leading to outright war. Downtown, with its date-palm-frond-covered souqs and its charming worn-out piazzas, where I spent much of my childhood, became the battleground. Combatants fought alley to alley, house to house, room to room, exactly as the dictator they'd toppled foretold. As the fighting spread and intensified, civilians scurried to the outskirts, regrouped in clans, armed themselves to scavenge the failing state's remains. The city, built on a drained marshland, became a vista of ruin and conflagration, interrupted now and then by shimmering lagoons formed from the broken sewer system and seawater overflow. The fighting has ended, but the ruins will likely remain ruins for a long time to come. As I watch the footage now, I notice reeds several feet high, young date palms and eager eucalyptus trees rising among the rubble of bombed-out modern towers and squat mud-walled homes.

A scruffy opulence
veils the ruins green. Nests
and birdsong to soothe

the mind's exhausted surf. Trees
can console.
But not enough.

PSALM FOR THE MEDICS

The road to paradise, an avalanche
        of blood, swerves away
    from them.

They hear a breath,
      launch their sirens
    through piled towers, blinding dust,

shovel to concrete-muffled moans—
       O eyes, heed—
    bodies snapped into silence—

Blow, mouth, into beaten lungs!
       Even God had to light the clay
    with his cold breath—

Hand, slap the new, tender flesh—
       Fingers, snatch a cry
    from the lifeless umbilical cord—

'ALAMS FOR TRIPOLI NIGHTS

deep in
   sleep above
      the sunrise

to move so far
   to note that one
      has not moved

a rumble
   climbing
      up the sky

are the stars
   happy
      in their caves

a call
   that sutures
      your dreams

are they
   alive when
      they blink

IV.

Fugitive Atlas

Traveler, where are you heading?
You embark, take sick and return.
So many innocents like you and me
were duped and lost their way.

Dahmane El-Harrachi

Ours be the tossing—wild though the sea—
Rather than a Mooring—unshared by thee.

Emily Dickinson

PSALM FOR DEPARTURE

Locusts wrap the sun in gauze,
the river swallows its banks.
No pleasure but seeing the no-

king crop here, the no-fields,
a petrified forest where twins were slain.
Someone will follow a bird.

The work of fire never ends:
Jinn build cities of mirage,
the poor stand waiting by the shore.

Signs made of stardust and spider
thread. Any way you measure it,
the difference will be a road.

PSALM ON THE ROAD TO AGADEZ

Day and night traveled
to reach these shores—
West to North

East to North
North to North
to North to North

—your country
your savage country
where you are free!

CONSTANCE SONG

Wave, checkpoint, and dune—
the roads we tread.
Each day a ragged plastic cup.

People forget how to die
and loss befriends their lament
to a fog heavy as wings.

"Far away, somewhere,
I have a brother or a sister
in this world," my Blessing hums.

PSALM UNDER SIEGE

Speak the body's thrift, the blood
and breath sustained by a candle
flame, remembrances

encircle like moths. No seagulls
when fishermen return
empty-handed to Arwad.

Locust-ravaged Idlib fields,
the dry wells of Daraa. Candle
light or soul—what else to call

what remains alive in me, how
it shrinks like an iris blinded
by death's blazing noon.

PSALM FOR CROSSING NIMROZ

What is a mere grazer
to the world of the many
and contending,

to the jealous one
of this earth's drying grass?
What to them?

What to time and limb
spent this far, the wind
voracious, its mind aflame?

AGADEZ BLUES

No place, no money for the bed.
Je dors dans la rue, paid only the way—
even God can't see me here.

Police take your money
quand tu n'as pas d'argent—
even God can't hear me here.

Ils te palpent tout le corps
pour vérifier, palpent all your body—
even God can't save me here.

I pay 1300 franc go to Libye
mais le chauffeur, il est parti—
even God can't help me here.

Je n'ai plus rien pour manger.
Je n'ai plus rien pour dormir—
even God can't find me here.

'ALAMS FOR GHOUTA

jasmine water
    from the ancient well
        you whisper

rasping through
    barrels' roar
        killing's fog

your words
    I can no longer wait
        you wander streets

walls you lean on
    your snow eyes
        your countless sorrows

almost blind
    you climb to reach
        a deeper refuge

I pluck you from
    soil that bore you
        your root of song

CONSTANCE PSALM

Lord,
Your hand
saved me,

but another
snatched
my child from

my breast.
A succubus
angel wanders

the desert clouds,
swirls below
the sand.

Why, Lord?
For what did You
save me?

MALOUK'S ODE

I tap a few words to her on WhatsApp or Viber
to blot out the day. I bring my nose close to the screen
to smell the photos she sends. Selfies of her

by the gas stove, or the baby making a gesture,
a smile or a yawn or a cry. Sometimes a video
of an old song. She asks about the sea; it's calm

but the traffickers no show. She breaks me,
a softness that turns me dusk, I, the poet dissident
who labored to rephrase the nations' inflamed contract,

who roved the bone sculptures made governments,
the sanctuaries filled with fear-bright eyes,
my words monosyllabic, soft as sighs.

There was blindness in my game, my epic of home.
I hear the smugglers, their pupils shifting as if following
a maddened gull, some bootleg spasm and discharge.

A blindness that cannot stop seeing,
those eyes will keep shifting like this in their graves.
I see my spirit too, a plastic cloud drifting in the breeze.

With them is our last chance, for what?
From the village drying up to sand, the town without jobs,
the hands that never learned to write, the eyes that barely read,

the soul hunger stump and trade.
Am I writing my poem again?
Have I become the exile I so mock and detest?

How to walk this sea?
How to not believe that such is possible?
Arrived in Kufra, the cramped 4×4s,

the HiLux where spent bodies cling to wooden poles,
IVECOs hundred-packed swaying death's wave.
Emptied in the camp, divided between sheets of galvanize,

the courtyard littered—bottles, clothes, old photographs—
like some carnival bacchanal the night before,
a town facing massacre just fled.

An empty, once-crowded barracoon
where the signal is one ribbon strong.
It is from here that I send her all my love.

PSALM UNDER SIEGE

Speak me, speak the fuel
I tossed into the fire: my dead
daughter's bed and books.

Recall ancestors who raided
hovels, dug up stored grains
packed into perfect cones.

Speak phone flashlight,
bullet holes, droppings,
and tracks to cans, boxes,

sacks. Speak the stashed-
away, forgotten gifts of
the disappeared and fled.

TRIPOLI DAYS

If I sweep this floor,
hack this meat, pluck
these olives until

my palms bleed, what
outcome is postponed,
multiplied into my years?

And what if there's no
place, only harbors, no
pillow or window frame?

Only more space
for the sullen dream
to grow and digress.

TRAFFICKER SOLILOQUY

Don't fear their eyes. They came
to you, after all, they paid their way.
Oh, they'll kill you given the chance.

You are a key in the dicey maze
of their lives, you clamp the cruelest lock.
Your breath is as foul as theirs.

Sometimes you think you'd had enough
of this trade in death, so much life,
these knots of unsorted dreaming.

But the sea is calm again, bats circle
the tangerine grove, riding the sultry breeze.
Time to send another boat, perhaps.

What's her name? Constance or
Blessing, the one paying her fare in bed—
she'll be here when you return.

THE AFFARI

Someone reaping land, trading it
for a 4×4 or a shipload of gasoline,
each body trucked or shipped.

Something to the trafficker, rescue worker, boat mechanic,
driver, kidnapper, salesman, food exporter, tire repairman,
money changer, doctor, medicine man, volunteer.

For each house torn down or blown
up, each bullet-riddled school, each
clinic built, detention center overrun.

Something to the peace-
keeper, terrorist, jet-
drone bombing him.

A salary, a bribe,
a grant, a stipend,
a ransom, a fellowship.

BLESSING'S SONG

The hands of your
kin, pits of desire for
the pain of others, O poet friend.

Flogging pounding
prodding scalding
human flesh, O poet friend.

Is this the legacy
of your noble, long-
awaited revolt, my poet friend?

BY THE SHORES OF BEHRAM

Bombed-out building smoke,
shelled hospital dust,
what eyes see when closed.

Or steam from a whale's
spout seen on TV
for solace retrieved.

It's my own breath this cold
night, or small clouds from
yawning children's mouths

waiting for the Zodiac. In
the distance a ship heading
for the Bosporus blowing

prophetic exhaust. How high
it ascends, how soon
dispersed—before you

think of its name in the new
languages you've learned—away,
away, toward some loss.

WITH LINES TAKEN FROM WALT WHITMAN

The auctioneer in militia fatigues
pushes you aside to conduct his business.
He has twelve lined up:

of the bonds, fees, threats,
and the quintillion beneficiaries,
the revolving cycle of birth,

poverty, and abuse,
truly and steadily roll'd,
he knows nothing, or pretends.

Or how they ended up in his hands,
and whence they go—
only his small part in the trade.

Of the cunning tendons and nerves,
under the glare of searchlight beams—
how will they swim the pool of labor's excess?

What building site or garment floor?
No time to be stript, flakes of breast-muscle,
pliant backbone, good-sized arms and legs,

where they had been Tasered, slashed
and whipped: that you may see them—
nothing, or pretends.

But witness, you note how the living
eyes matte, the faces acumen-drained.
"Brothers, we have no time," he says.

Spare him talk of countless immortal lives
in parlors and lecture-rooms across
rich princedoms and Frontex states.

He knows within there runs blood,
same old blood. How easily it spills,
how evidence is hidden and drained.

Whatever the bids of the bidders,
none of your brothers
will exceed 100 quid.

FIRE AT SEA: A FUNERAL CHANT

"Fire at Sea" is the name of a migrant tragedy that occurred on the night of October 3rd, 2013, by the shore of the Italian island of Lampedusa. A boat carrying migrants that had set sail from Misrata, Libya, began to sink less than half a mile from the island. Passengers lit torches to seek help, but a fire ignited and ended up consuming the whole boat. Out of the more than 500 passengers on board, only 155 were rescued. The chant here refers to another migrant tragedy in 2015 where a passenger on a sinking dinghy pleads for help. The Italian Coast Guard who could not locate the boat kept asking him the same question, which now has come to pertain to all facets of what has been called the refugee crisis.

What's your position?

What's your position now, please?

Your position, please.

PSALM FOR THE BALKAN ROUTE

At peace in the palm: embers,
perfumes, the scents of Abyssinia
and Mecca haunt the brain.

You remember weddings and feasts.
Hail pocked the copper dust, and you,
open-mouthed, gazed at the world.

Years have passed since that since.
How does the body know how to pin
so much of itself in words?

SONG FOR AMADOU

Have you made it
to Sicily, Amadou?
Are you deep

in the woods of Denmark?
Learned a new language,
writing your book?

Have they put you on
a plane home, Amadou?
Kidnapped you, sent you back

to that camp in Bani Walid,
slaving day and night
on a farm for some crook?

Are you in paradise
now, Amadou?
A skeleton bleaching

in the desert,
a bloated corpse
on a sunny beach?

THE BOAT MERCHANT'S WIFE

—Sabratha

He started out making feluccas;
an Egyptian taught him how.
Then he opened a shop by the beach,

sold ice cream, parasols, and chairs.
His mother asked for my hand when
I was in teacher college, first year.

Time passes like the Ghibli here.
I was seven months with my third baby
when someone sought him

for a Zodiac. He traveled all the way
to Guangzhou, brought back a dozen,
has been selling them ever since.

One night I asked how strong
they were, how many they carry.
"It's all in the booklet," he said,

"no reason for what keeps happening
to them." He sipped from a glass
of bokha and explained how

from this same jetty, long before
the Arabs and Vandals, even before
the Romans and their famous theater,

boats filled with people and goods
and sailed off. A day or a week later,
the sea sends back the drowned.

His long-lashed eyes closed when
he spoke, his face unchanged by the years.
His fingers moved so carefully

putting out his cigarette. He saw me
looking, nodded, then pulled me toward
his manhood to help him sleep.

INTO THE SEA

Barely out of the jetty, the boat rises
with every wave, and from the back
two or three fall into the sea.

At sunset the boat starts to lose
air, fills with water, mothers
and babies fall into the sea.

One side stays afloat. We cling
to a rope, water up to our bellies
and people fall into the sea.

All night we grip and bleed.
Rain so cold, waves five stories high.
If only I could fall into the sea.

Sunrise, a helicopter. I find
a red shirt, wave it to them.
They watch us fall into the sea.

They fling a small inflatable boat.
I am too weak to reach it.
Others try and fall into the sea.

A cargo boat throws a rope
to get us on board. Alive at last,
and we still fall into the sea.

FUEL BURNS

Gasoline canisters leak
or get knocked over;
gasoline mixes with seawater,

and when the mixture
touches human skin,
skin begins to burn.

Women sitting in the bottom
or the center of the boat
are at highest risk.

Dinghies are fitted
with plywood floors
fixed with nails and screws

that puncture people's feet.
The wood soaks up water,
expands, and then splits.

Women and children often
fall through the floor
or are trampled and drown.

People fight on the boat,
the bodies of survivors
and the dead are full

of scratches, bite marks,
cuts, and bruises, but it's
fuel burns that horrify most.

Survivors arrive
hypothermic, dehydrated,
barely conscious.

They must shower
with soap to get relief,
and need help stripping off

their fuel-soaked clothes, but
just touching their clothing
can make latex gloves melt.

PSALM FOR ARRIVAL

When we find the sounds
for words we need, their death
rattle begins to echo in our throats.

Memory creeps up on old sentiments,
finds them lurking like blind fish
in the twilight of our blood.

Dead and living on—ancient prophecies
or frozen microbes—something we disavow
continues to feed on us.

MALOUK'S QASSIDA

Lampedusa only a dozen leagues now, the bay
between it and Sousse a corridor of debris,
a Phoenician graveyard.

Are we prepared for the storm's paradise?
The starlings recite the Zodiacs on their wings;
the marabouts must in kindness abide.

On the wireless the noises of rescue—
the double dealing of virtue and abuse—
into a theater of salvation we ride.

We are exalted into some hippopotamus,
our mouths checked, hands gloved
with inhuman skin, their fingers inside.

The mouths that speak are covered like Tuaregs',
the eyes swathed with a dusky mirage.
Our names taken, flicker like fireflies.

Looped around our wrists, numbers
that look like a kind of price.
The bullhorns cry, the seagulls deride.

On slippery bridges, we're wrapped in gold foil,
woozy, often diseased. But who is saving whom?
The question's not stated, only implied.

MORIA JOURNAL

About you
a grave
yard

on this
much
that

the that
you live
in

the this
much you
live on

the all
about you
a grave

a yard or
two the
not much

the yes
you are
one too.

DETERRENCE

Give them enough,
but not food
they like. Never

deny rumors
about pork.
Make sure

there's a lot
of soap but you
can skimp

on water. Don't
ever repair
windows,

never enough
blankets or
socks or shoes.

No diapers for
weeks, one sanitary
napkin per day.

HORGOS-RÖSZKE JOURNAL

Sign says
We will
let you

abandoned
stadia shipping
containers

your children
darting
about

lice
bed bugs
rats.

QASSIDA TO THE STATUE OF SAPPHO IN MYTILINI

Kyria, why do you stand askance, facing neither
    sea nor mountain,
not even toward your wildflower fields?

And the lyre on your shoulder, was it meant
    to be the size
of the plastic jugs shouldered by Moria's refugees?

I saw them in Sicily too, home of your exile,
    where no rescue
could pause time's grating at their memories.

Your island is empty of poets, Kyria. I came
    to meet them,
to recall the trembling earth under my feet.

Hangers-on reporting to newsletters throng
    the cafés, researchers
hacking at fieldwork, polishing CVs.

The migrants are all court poets now. At night
    they labor to
translate their traumas into EU legalese.

Or sit at your feet shouting into cell phones
    to scattered relatives,
trying to crack the code of the model asylee.

Kyria, there's no way for me to see you, no date
    or sculptor's name,
only fascist graffiti below your knees.

Why do your eyes glare lifeless like apricot pits,
    your stone body dim,
a paper lamp trembling in the breeze?

Or is that you now, Kyria, wearing hijab,
    holding Cleis's hand,
glad to be home again, but not quite at ease?

'ALAMS FOR ROBERT HAYDEN

was it discipline
   or self-love
      brought us

a number
   a listing
      a teenager

sacrifice
   a bleary rain
      insolvent

a bathroom wall
   some web page
      prostitute

self-hate
   a harmattan
      upon these shores

in Catania
   Allah is great
      Jesus is love

PROCREATION

Dreams copulate
with our memories. We begin
to have many days of birth,

many mothers. Our fathers'
names branch out like weeds
God shatters countless like stars.

Don't close your eyes,
or the stories you've told
will swallow you.

Look to your body:
Your skin will be your anchor.
Your scars will never betray you.

CURSE TABLET

—Calais

who conquer   virgin continents
who squat   on burial grounds
who sleep   murderous sleep

who taint   with spells
who fertilize   poisoned seed
what drink   what eat

what curse   split oceans
what manna   from hell sky
to feed   what greed

blood smears   hands arms
vengeance ink   inscribed in rules
endowed war   the peace you keep

PSALM OF THE VOLUNTEER

—For the rescuers and volunteers in Lesbos

Dear world,
who am I to
condemn you?

Dear eyes,
who am I to
blind you?

Dear lies,
who am I to
chastise you?

Dear ignorance,
who am I to
float above you?

Dear hypocrisy,
who am I to claim
not to know you?

Dear self-
righteousness, how
am I to subdue you?

Dear soul,
who am I to
shun you?

Dear soul,
who am I to
shelter you?

Dear soul,
how am I
to repair you?

PSALM FOR THE DEPARTED

A fistful of myrrh in his left
hand, and his farewell wave
is the Bennu's heavenward flight.

His voice a thread buried
in sand, an incandescent light
inflaming a sky gleaming

with ink. He'll be pure and I will
stand an inexplicable glyph
waiting to be assigned.

Measure now your heart's
contraband—all that's delved
between us. Measure it

in blood. Tell the mind to
withstand what it's discounted
but could never disavow.

AFTERWARD BREATHING

we have   after
    children   the
    born here   sea

now   still
    at night we   at
    watch them   sea

to learn   under
    from their   the
    breathing   sea

V.

What have we to do with nothingness, we who are mortal?

Yves Bonnefoy

BEATITUDE

She speaks to me in our language
in front of her friends, to share a secret,
or—cool and beaming—to show off.

I wonder how long it will last, this pride,
this intimacy. Sometimes she puts her arm
next to mine and tells me I have the lighter skin.

"Why are you doing this?" I ask.
But she doesn't point to the flag
or say, "It's the way of the world."

Instead she tells me not to worry, that she is "the most
kid kid in my class, the least mature one, Baba!"
Not all kinds of wisdom console, I tell her.

Then I begin to think of words she'll soon hear
that can make her wish she wasn't who she is.
Lead me to virtue, O love, through the smoke of despair.

AFTER CHARLOTTESVILLE

For days after—this was always coming—
            muscles taut to the smell
      of first arrival—the scent of an old fire

in the woods. "Pioneers," Naipaul called them,
            maddened and bearing torches,
                  "a primitivism borne of civilization itself."

A friend who once tended to Jefferson's foxgloves
                  comes to mind as you watch
            the streamed movie to see

the great actor express—what is the Arabic word
            for déjà vu? A dream released
                  from restrictive facts. A murderer's face

of indifference—the mind desperate
                  to see things anew. You want a picture—
      the obsession with ancestry like a tangle of boughs—

Pound's boughs—Mussolini
            hung upside down—the boughs
                  covered with snow—dripping blood.

You want footage of the cigarette break,
                  soldiers smoking after
      the bodies had been hauled from the gas chamber.

You look at your roof and wonder if it's time
            to install solar panels. Surely,
                  this is not your first encounter

with this sort of thing? The immigration
                  officer says, "Welcome home!"
      Somehow it sounded like,

"Welcome to my home." You remember the face
            of the butcher's assistant.
                        You'd gone to the shop

and picked a lamb from the pen in the back—
            yes, the lamb—it was braying,
            "clover, clover," and in fifteen minutes—

what do you call an animal's body after
            it's slaughtered and skinned?—
                        strange there isn't an English word

for that—considering. The innards, heart, lung, and liver
            in a plastic bag if you wanted them.
            And the blood? The blood is—déjà vu—

and it's always Othello's—how in Aleppo once,
            I took by the throat the circumcised dog,
                        and smote him,

thus. Desdemona lies sleeping in D. W. Griffith's arms.
            That's why these woods
            are no longer mere background.

The scent of an old rapture and the enigma
            of a current buried in the spine.
                        Of course, he can say "Welcome!"

if it's his decision to let you in or not.
                        But that's not the only difference
            between *displace* and *replace*. Their flags

emblazoned with axes and saws announce
            a new kind of math. A new look
                        for the old machinery droning

to convince you it's your people who are sick
                        in the head. As you drove away, you saw
            the man who transfigured

the lamb. All cleaned up, hair combed—
        almost smell the soap
                on his hands—waiting for the microbus

home. "Maybe someday you'll go
                to college here," you tell your daughter
        as you enter Monticello.

"It's time to donate your old car
        to the radio station," she instructs you.
                Looking at photographs of lynchings,

your eyes avert the martyrs' unbearable holiness
                and you gaze and gaze
        at the leering, familiar faces.

THE SUBURBS

In the backyard, I see him standing among the trees, bow in hand, a stone axe strapped to his waist. He is exploring a land no one owned yet, feeling emotions that had not been felt for a long time here. He does not see me, and I can only see him through the eyes of a word that started out moving slowly, reaching for something far away, then seizing it in a fist. Linger, long, belong, so goes the history of dispossession.

The leaves fall and drift, gather and swirl as if they are a murmuration of starlings and the front-yard a piece of sky. The chipmunks darting under the hostas may have a better explanation, but they seem too impatient to give it. But him, what brings him here now, deep from history? Is he bringing us awful news? Has he come to rescue us? I want to tell him that he can have it all, that everything here is a weight tied to my feet, that it pulls me despite myself into forms of disquiet I had never known.

See, how I've opted to let the dandelions bully the grass, I want to tell him, how I let the grass grow disheveled beyond polite length, how a thin film of mold is turning the northern side of our white-painted house green! Is this how I'm giving it all back?

I want also to tell him that when it rains in the spring, our sodden backyard becomes a virtual bog, our failed rain garden a small lagoon. Some nights deer stop by to drink. Frogs live there now; Canada geese alight, wet their beaks and soak their wings.

What will snatch them from
the justice of twigs and branches?
A specter haunts

the hush, a phantom dark; their
nests
catch the light, flare up in sparks.

AT WESTGATE MALL, NAIROBI

—In memoriam Kofi Awoonor

Maestro, we went there,
sought the same Indian
restaurant, ordered food

we imagined you'd want to eat.
We bought local tea
for friends, and my wife

bought me a blue
paisley shirt for our
anniversary. All the while

we looked for places to hide,
places where you may
have tried to hide. Two nights

ago my daughter asked
what *shahada* meant,
then what *shahid* meant.

And because she loves to sing
she recited the Fatiha and
Surat al-'Asr.

I do not know when
I'll tell her that that
would not have saved us,

that we, I pray and hope,
would not have wanted to be
saved without you.

Forgive me for keeping her
innocent a little longer.
Soon enough she'll

understand. I promise to read
her your "Grains and Tears"
when her time of courage comes.

'ALAMS FOR SUN ON SHUTTERED WINDOWS

—For the young writers, and for Laila and her family

how has
    this burden
        lived as dead

pushed
    you swerve
        the way ahead

the sky a hole
    at your feet
        earth overhead

you dream
    to ravish
        the purebred

given up
    your child
        your lover

your face
    stranger
        silenced unheard

one's
    life only
        one's grief

where there's no
    sweetness to
        your strife

you stray
    roads pull out
        their knives

their smugness
    calcified
        deception

history or future
    a weight
        you won't shed

how you long to
    live another
        life in your life

everywhere
    a hemorrhage
        of dread

legend
    grasp
        only to shed

everywhere
    a hemorrhage
        of dread

undone by light
    shadows
        torn to shreds

everywhere
    a hemorrhage
        of dread

see a
    book
        read and reread

A FRIEND FROM AL-RAQQA

I'm remembering now a friend from Al-Raqqa. Studying to become an agricultural engineer when I first met him, he couldn't wait to graduate and go home. I used to chide him, saying, "You'll be returning to the Great Leader. It'll be Revolution this and Motherland that for you from now on." He'd play along with a send-up of Baath party bureaucrats stuttering through their allegiance oaths. Then he'd quickly turn to me and say, "But you know you're the one who's trapped. Can't stay here, can't go there," which was true then. He was returning to his Euphrates, to the family farm with a notebook full of plans and a head buzzing with dreams. We exchanged letters several times early on, I still remember his address:

P. O. Box ##
Al-Raqqa City, Syria

He sent back postcards of the river, and news of his farm, his fields of clover and herds of sheep. "It's paradise here," he wrote soon after he got married. "We started a bee nursery," he reported once, and later, "We just exported our first shipment of fig preserve to the Emirates. ORGANIC 100%!" "You just have to keep your focus despite all the hurdles, and you'll succeed even here," one of his last letters closed.

Our lives took different and more entangled paths by our early thirties, and I did not hear from him for more than twenty years, not until a year ago. His city and mine, surged in hope then fell into nightmare. ISIS took his farm, he wrote from Damascus. He managed to ship the children off to study abroad, Canada, Turkey, Greece, likely never to return. "I have so much time on my hands now. I translate two short stories a week, and newspaper articles, several every day. I probably translate in my sleep."

Al-Raqqa is now mile upon mile of rubble, the destruction mainly the work of American fighter jets. What remains standing is probably booby-trapped. When it rains in the countryside near his farm—the rain now comes from different directions, my friend tells me—"the old huts and barns are mounds of glistening clay."

Words drench garden and reeds.

It'll soon burst, the dirt taut
with seeds.
Thirst that grips my heart.

WE ARE SAYING "YES," BUT WHO ARE WE TO SAY?

That silence again
        a wall
of feathers, and near

enough
        to block the
circuit of our time—

adobe wall,
        roads of dust—
thirty-two years

until the bones
        discoursed—
that's how long

I've dug into
        myself—
and the baby?

She is a promise—
        ungraspable,
mist—

fuss or no fuss,
        yearn, yearn,
yearn. Heart

pounds, ears
        throb—
will it ask

the question
        tattooed
on our skin?

Until dirt
         fills
my eyes, you say.

Call it wait
         or rest—the stare,
the lunge back

into what we can't
         swim—
another shore now—

how our arms flail
         the joints'
acidic burn—

a hunger
         unbeknown
to us, a flame cupped

in skin—Oh anticipant,
         Oh dear
loving Lord—to hold

a burden like a need
         and let
a new life begin.

THE ONLY ONE WE HAVE

Scientists have been studying the skeleton of one of our ancestors who was about forty when he died. His skull shows that he suffered a serious injury to the left side of his head as a teenager, an injury so severe that he was most likely blind and otherwise disabled. As he matured, the right side of his body began to atrophy while the left side, being fed by the right brain, continued to develop. He could walk, but with a limp. The bones on his right leg and arm weakened and shortened; his right hand eventually shriveled to nothing. What is surprising is that he lived for at least two decades after his injury, which could have occurred while hunting a large mammal, or in one of the turf wars he and his clan fought against their competitors. Scientists are certain, given his blindness and the severe headaches he must have suffered from his head trauma, this particular ancestor could not have existed without other people taking care of him for two decades. His remains were discovered in a cave a few hundred miles north of Baghdad. From the pollen found near his skeleton, scientists hypothesize that flowers had been buried with him as with the others lying next to him.

> In the cave lit by
> a sputtering flame, they feed
> him summer's blue light,
>
> their hands rough with rank
>   rare flowers;
> the sweet sea's loves and hours.

'ALAMS FOR CAIRO NIGHTS

—After Gertrude Stein and Oum Kalthoum

I can't bear to blink
   I can't bear
      the absence

I can't wallow
   I can't bear
      this is how hard

this is how much
   with a word
      so much is said

a word like you
   where are they
      where can one look

I hear it
   but it burns
      and burns like a song

I want to talk to you
   in a way that's open
      I want to talk to you

a way that multiplies
   that binds our love
      with words

a word like you
   where in secret
      where love tries

I can't yield
   to the absence
      of your breath

behind my lids
   bear such waste
      your breath disarmed

a word not said
   a word like this love
      a word unsaid

a word like breath
   such words unbirthed
      a word now lost

a love that burns
   a song that says
      that says and stays

in all the ways
   in secret
      in the ways I never talk

in secret
   a kind of music
      we try to catch

a word
   is caught
      to catch its words

to close my eyes
   not even for a second
      disarmed

this is how bad
   this is how much
      how dark it gets

a word
   in tenderness
      lost its breath

like love
   unbound
      nowhere found

never burned out
   a heart still breathes
      a love unbound

I don't talk
   that talk
      even in secret

with others' secrets
   we try to catch
      our breath

I can't talk
   a word where love is
      and is caught

OUR CITIES

When I think of our cities, it's always siesta time decades ago. Our houses had no phones, and the one television channel didn't start until early evening. There was nothing to do but to sneak out to a neighbor's house or to read or join the adults in their sleep. A time of conspiracies and devastating change—the photo of Mossadagh in pajamas after his nap receiving news of the Shah's impending return, and Nasser, already broken, listening to a report about Black September. But also a time of new music, poetry, and film, of women teachers teaching eager girls, of setting aside myths for the sake of a modest dream. A promise conceived in quiet assurance tossed into history's profane embrace.

Now it's the mayhem and clangor of descent: your city roaring like God revving up an old, tired engine; Bassam's city and its harlotry of renewal where the temporary crusts into the eternal; and Hassan's city of convulsions and dark cloisters where clerics plot the savior's return. All have their counterparts here in America. O how they long to bring the world to an end, to ascend to their Lord like laser beams before the missiles are unleashed!

When we left home, we thought we were joining "the immense city composed of two words: the others," where "in every one of them there is an *I* clipped from a *we*," the metropolis "that dreams us all, that all of us build and unbuild and rebuild as we dream."

I see you smiling at my child, in both your eyes a glimmer that redeems.

But I have news for you. In your city of exile, they're building an elevated park meant to protect it from the new fierce storms and rising seas. A series of levees and a floodwall, the park will add eleven blocks of green space with biking and jogging trails, a theater, a gallery, restaurants and cafés. This project too will shortchange nearby neighborhoods. It's meant only to protect the financial district and the high-income high-risers living near.

All who wear a mortal
mould rise as the sun their
father rose. Let it

gird, not break, your heart: the world's
amends:
the toil imposed.

BEATITUDE

"Let's walk through the woods," she tells me.
"Let's walk by the rocky shore at sunrise."
"Let's walk through the clover fields at noon."

In the rainforest she is silent, mesmerized.
She'd never prayed—we never taught her—
but she seemed to then, eyes alert with joy.

She points to a chameleon the size of a beetle,
teaches me the names of flowers and trees,
insects we can eat if we're ever lost here.

"I'm teaching you how to entrust the world
to me," she says. "You don't have to live
forever to shield me from it."

NOTES

Shikwah: The title word is the Urdu for complaint (from the Arabic *shakwa*). It is the title of a poem by the great Indian poet Muhammad Iqbal (1877–1938). A complaint to God, the poem bemoans the state of the poet's people, his Muslim brethren, and the decline of their civilization. Attacked for writing a sacrilegious text, Iqbal wrote a follow-up poem titled *Jawab-e-Shikwah* ("Reply to the Complaint") in which God presumably answers the poet, instructing him that He has not broken His promise to the faithful; rather it is they who failed to follow the straight path, which led to their decline and humiliation. Not a speaker or reader of Urdu or Farsi (in which Iqbal wrote most of his poems), I encountered the poem first in the form of Oum Kalthoum's song *Hadith al-Rouh* ("Dialogue of Souls"), which is based on Ahmad Rami's Arabic translation of Iqbal's poem.

A Dream of Adam: The form of this piece, and several others in this book that take the same shape, is a modified haibun that ends with a renga rather than a haiku. The renga here incorporates lines from John Milton's *Paradise Lost* (Book X) and Alfred Lord Tennyson's "Tithonus."

Season of Migration to the North: The title of this poem is the same as Tayeb Salih's masterpiece *Mausim al-Hijrah ilâ al-Shamâl* (*Season of Migration to the North*).

Plume: The prose passage on the city of Ann Arbor's toxic plume is based on numerous reports on the subject. The renga that concludes this haibun combines lines from Algernon Charles Swinburne's "A Ballad of François Villon, Prince of All Ballad-Makers," Jennifer Elise Foerster's poem "Coosa," and the Egyptian *Book of the Dead*.

'Alams for Saying "Yes": 'Alams are short poems composed and chanted by Bedouin poets of eastern Libya and western Egypt. Unrhymed short phrases, 'alams are pithy statements often quoted in daily conversation to express an individual's immediate circumstances. 'Alams are also called *ghinaywat* ("little songs"). See Lila Abu-Lughod's *Veiled Sentiments: Honor and Poetry in a Bedouin Society* (University of California Press, 1986).

Unreal City: The renga that concludes this haibun combines lines from Lollie Butler's "The Comfort Women" and May Sayigh's "Lament."

Occupation: An Index: The various tercets that make up this poem include many found and untraceable sources along with statements, lines, and passages from Patrice Lumumba, King Baudouin of Belgium, Joseph Conrad's *Heart of Darkness*, Amira Hass, Golda Meir, Rajab Buhwaish, James Joyce's *Ulysses*, Homi Bhabha, Aimé Césaire, Raphael Patai, Dennis Brutus, Rafael Eitan, Frantz Fanon, and the book of Joshua.

Our Neighbors: Poisoned City: To compose this account of the Flint water crisis, I have relied on Anna Clark's excellent book *The Poisoned City: Flint's Water and the American Urban Tragedy* (Metropolitan Books, 2018), from which I also borrowed the title of my piece. The renga at the end combines lines from Charles Baudelaire's poem "Poison" and William Blake's "A Poison Tree."

Face: The story of the wounded Marine and the photograph taken of him and his bride told in sections 2 and 9 is a slightly fictionalized account of a true story. Section 4: Iraq saw a huge rise in birth defects (including babies with two heads) during the first Iraq war and the American invasion of the country in 2003. More recently, "dramatic increases in infant mortality, cancer and leukemia in the Iraqi city of Fallujah, which was bombarded by US Marines in 2004, exceed those reported by survivors of the atomic bombs that were dropped on Hiroshima and Nagasaki in 1945, according to a new study," reports the *Independent* newspaper of London. Section 10 is indebted to Amiri Baraka's poem "Something in the Way of Things."

An Idea for a Short Film: The renga that concludes this haibun combines lines from Shakespeare's Sonnet 71 and Thomas Campion's "Now Winter Nights Enlarge."

'Alams from the Black Horse Prison, Tripoli, Circa 1981: This sequence of 'alams is based on a speech by Dr. Thomas Stockmann in Henrik Ibsen's play *An Enemy of the People*. El-Mufti and Al-Shaltami, a medical doctor and a poet respectively, were both political prisoners in the Black Horse prison in Libya in the 1980s. El-Mufti recounts how at some point he heard a radio performance of the aforementioned Ibsen play on the BBC and how the play was inspirational and sustaining for him. This 'alam sequence tries to imagine El-Mufti translating this particular speech to his great friend Al-Shaltami, and the poet, who wrote in classical Arabic and the colloquial Libyan dialect, turning Stockmann's speech into a sequence of 'alams.

Now That We Have Tasted Hope: This poem was written at the beginning of the Libyan uprising against Muammar Al-Qaddafi in February 2011. The phrase "bread of bitterness" is from Claude McKay's "America."

Your City: The renga at the end of this haibun combines lines from Percy Bysshe Shelley's "Ozymandias" and Amal Dunqul's *Safar al-Takween* ("The Book of Creation").

After 42 Years (Revisited): This poem includes passages from a short story written by Muammar Al-Qaddafi titled *Al-huroob ila al-jahim* ("Escape to Hell").

My City: The renga that concludes this haibun combines lines from Su Croll's "the consolation of trees" and Derek Walcott's "Sea Grapes."

Malouk's Ode: Malouk is a character, who is a poet, in Abu Bakr Kahal's novel *African Titanics*, translated by Charis Bredin (Darf Publishers, London, 2017).

Tripoli Days: This poem borrows an image from Derek Walcott's "The Schooner *Flight*."

Trafficker Soliloquy: This poem borrows several images from Robert Hayden's "Middle Passage."

By the Shores of Behram: Zodiacs are the inflatable rubber boats used by migrants in sea-crossing journeys.

With Lines Taken from Walt Whitman: Various phrases are borrowed from Walt Whitman's "I Sing the Body Electric." Frontex is the European Border and Coast Guard Agency.

Fuel Burns: This poem is an erasure of a blog entry by Dr. Sarah Giles, a Canadian physician who volunteered for Doctors Without Borders in the Central Mediterranean in 2016. I am grateful to Dr. Giles for allowing me to create a poem out of her text.

Moria Journal: This poem refers to the Moria Refugee Camp located on the outskirts of Mytilini on the island of Lesbos in Greece.

Horgos-Röszke Journal: This poem refers to the prison-style, government-run, refugee detention center in the town of Röszke in Hungary near the border with Serbia where refugees are housed in shipping containers. In 2017, the Hungarian parliament passed a law that allows the government to lock up all asylum seekers in detention camps until their cases are decided on, which often takes months. The law also permits police to return asylum seekers from anywhere in the country back to Serbia.

'Alams for Robert Hayden: These poems borrow several phrases from Robert Hayden's "Middle Passage."

The Suburbs: The renga that concludes this haibun combines lines from George Oppen's "The Gesture" and Bakiza Amin Khaki's *Ya Qalb* ("O Heart").

At Westgate Mall, Nairobi: Kofi Awoonor (1935–2013) was one of the giants of African poetry, as well as a literary critic, professor of comparative literature, and an ambassador for his native Ghana. He was killed in the Westgate shopping mall attack in Kenya in September 2013. The poem "Grains and Tears" can be found in the poet's last book, *The Promise of Hope: New and Selected Poems, 1964–2013* (University of Nebraska Press, 2014).

'Alams for Sun on Shuttered Windows: In the summer of 2017, my colleague Laila Moghrabi and I published an anthology of young Libyan writers titled *Shams 'ala Nawafidh Mughlaqa*

(*Sun on Shuttered Windows*). The 500-page anthology contained short stories, poetry, and prose by twenty-five Libyan writers, all under thirty-five, as well as two essays by prominent Libyan literary critics. It was published by Darf Publishers, London. The book was meant to launch a new generation of Libyan writers to their nation, which had been embroiled in civil strife since the death of Muammar Al-Qaddafi in 2011. Two months after publication and a generally positive reception to the book, a fierce campaign instigated by Islamic extremists erupted on the internet. The outrage was mainly directed at one selection from the anthology that depicted a sexual encounter. Almost everyone involved in the book received death threats and insults that numbered in the thousands. Laila and other women contributors received a disproportionate share of the public shaming and threats. Fearing for their lives, some of the writers hid with their families, changed residences, or left the country. Laila left Libya with her family shortly after the attack and has not returned since then. These 'alams are dedicated to all the contributors in the book, and to all writers working in extreme circumstances.

A Friend from Al-Raqqa: The last three lines in this haibun are based on lines from "Tracing" by Gottfried Benn, translated from the German by Michael Hofmann.

The Only One We Have: The renga that concludes this haibun combines lines from Cathy Song's "Kindness" and Swinburne's "The Triumph of Time."

'Alams for Cairo Nights: The 'alams of this poem are based on the lyrics of Oum Kalthoum's song "Amal Hayati." Lyrics by Ahmad Shafiq Kamal, music composed by Mohamed Abdel Wahab.

Our Cities: The prose passage of this haibun includes lines from Octavio Paz's "I Speak of the City," and the renga reworks lines from Shelley's "The Triumph of Life." The characters I refer to here are all from Tamer El-Said's film *In the Last Days of the City*.

ACKNOWLEDGMENTS

I am grateful to A. Van Jordan, Fady Joudah, William Olsen, Arthur Sze, Lyn Hejinian, Rabih Alameddine, Hayan Charara, and Eugene Gloria for offering encouraging feedback and numerous suggestions on earlier drafts of this manuscript.

I would like to thank the MacArthur Foundation and the University of Michigan for their generous support of my work.

Some of these poems were written or revised during a residency at the University of Arizona Poetry Center.

I wish also to thank the editors of these magazines where some of the poems in this manuscript have been published:

The Arkansas International: Psalm for Departure; Psalm under Siege 1; Agadez Blues; Tripoli Days.

Artful Dodge: Psalm for the Balkan Road; Psalm for Crossing Nimroz; By the Shores of Behram; Psalm under Siege 2; Deterrence.

Beloit Poetry Journal: Now That We Have Tasted Hope.

Boston Review: At Westgate Mall, Nairobi; Beatitudes 1–4; 'Alams for Sun on Shuttered Windows; 'Alams for Cairo Nights; 'Alams from the Black Horse Prison, Tripoli, Circa 1981.

Colorado Review: Face.

Consequence: A Story.

Copper Nickel: Procreation.

Fifth Wednesday: Season of Migration to the North; Into the Sea; Song for Amadou.

Harper's Magazine: Psalm under Siege 1.

Image Journal: A Dream of Adam; Plume; Unreal City; Our Neighbors: Poisoned City; An Idea for a Short Film; My City; A Friend from Al-Raqqa; Your City; The Suburbs; The Only One We Have; Our Cities.

The Iowa Review: Psalm on the Road to Agadez; Constance Song; Constance Psalm; Blessing's Song; The Affari; Fire at Sea: Funeral Chant; Trafficker Soliloquy; Curse Tablet; Horgos-Röszke Journal; Afterward Breathing.

The Kenyon Review: Qassida to the Statue of Sappho in Mytilini; Fuel Burns; Malouk's Ode; Moria Journal; Psalm of the Volunteer.

Los Angeles Times: After 42 Years.

Making Mirrors: Writing/Righting by and for Refugees, edited by Jehan Bseiso and Becky Thompson, Interlink Press: Psalm for Arrival; Psalm for the Balkan Route; Psalm for the Medics.

The Mighty Stream: Poems in Celebration of Martin Luther King, edited by Carolyn Forché and Jackie Kay, Bloodaxe Press, UK: Anthropocene Hymns.

Mizna: Occupation: An Index.

New England Review: Malouk's Qassida; Psalm for the Departed.

Poem-a-Day: Shikwah.

Poetry: The Boat Merchant's Wife.

Poetry Now: We Are Saying "Yes," but Who Are We to Say?

Several of the poems in section IV of this book have appeared as a chapbook titled *Mare Nostrum*, published by Sarabande Books, 2019.

KHALED MATTAWA has published four full volumes and a chapbook of poetry. He has translated volumes of Arabic poetry and has edited anthologies of Arab American writing. Recipient of a MacArthur Fellowship, and a former Chancellor of the Academy of American Poets, Mattawa is the William Wilhartz Endowed Professor of English Language and Literature at the University of Michigan, where he edits *Michigan Quarterly Review*.

The text of *Fugitive Atlas* is set in Garamond Premier Pro.
Book design by Rachel Holscher.
Composition by Bookmobile Design and Digital Publisher Services,
Minneapolis, Minnesota.
Manufactured by Versa Press on acid-free, 30 percent postconsumer wastepaper.